F*ck You Haiku

F*ck You Haiku

*Little Breakup Poems to Help You
Vent, Heal, and Move On*

Kristina Grish

TILLER PRESS
New York London Toronto Sydney New Delhi

An Imprint of Simon & Schuster, Inc.
1230 Avenue of the Americas
New York, NY 10020

First Tiller Press hardcover edition January 2021

TILLER PRESS and colophon are trademarks of Simon & Schuster, Inc.

For information about special discounts for bulk purchases,
please contact Simon & Schuster Special Sales at 1-866-506-1949 or
business@simonandschuster.com.

The Simon & Schuster Speakers Bureau can bring authors to your live
event. For more information or to book an event, contact the
Simon & Schuster Speakers Bureau at 1-866-248-3049 or visit our
website at www.simonspeakers.com.

Interior design by Jennifer Chung

Manufactured in the United States of America

1   3   5   7   9   10   8   6   4   2

Library of Congress Cataloging-in-Publication Data

Names: Grish, Kristina, author.
Title: F*ck you haiku : little breakup poems to help you vent, heal,
and move on / Kristina Grish. | Other titles: Fuck you haiku |
Description: New York : Tiller Press, 2021. | Identifiers: LCCN
2020034572 (print) | LCCN 2020034573 (ebook) |
ISBN 9781982157975 (hardcover) | ISBN 9781982157982 (ebook) |
Subjects: LCSH: Dating (Social customs)—Humor. | Man-woman
relationships—Humor. | Separation (Psychology)—Humor. |
Haiku, American. | Classification: LCC PN6231.D3 G745 2021 (print) |
LCC PN6231.D3 (ebook) | DDC 811/.6—dc23

LC record available at https://lccn.loc.gov/2020034572
LC ebook record available at https://lccn.loc.gov/2020034573

ISBN 978-1-9821-5797-5
ISBN 978-1-9821-5798-2 (ebook)

To Gena, who always gets it.
I love you, sis.

You crushed my sweet soul

And forced me to haiku you

Who gets the last laugh?

Contents

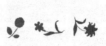

Preface

One crisp, fall afternoon, my husband of twelve years asked me out on a lunch date. I was excited to spend time with him, just the two of us, as we'd been living separately for the past few months due to the fact that I was sick with a frightening and unwieldy illness and being in our house made me feel physically worse. We'd made a promise to each other that we would put our place on the market in the spring, after preparing it to sell, and then finally reunite under a healthier roof. Our son was six years old at the time and especially excited to go house hunting so that we could once again be together as a happy little family.

All our plans came to a screeching halt, however, when my husband rushed into the pub where we'd agreed to meet for lunch, insisting that we talk in the parking lot. He was anxious and wild-eyed. I worried that something was wrong with our child or with my husband's mom, who was babysitting him that day.

"I've filed for divorce," the supposed love of my life

nervously blurted out. "You'll be hearing from my lawyer this week. I've been planning this for six months."

Wait, *what*?

I'll be hearing from *whom*?

Somehow, I'd come to the restaurant for a veggie burger and friendly conversation but was about to leave with a wrecked marriage and a confused, broken heart.

Needless to say, I was completely blindsided by this stealthy and devastating turn of events. I immediately burst into tears—a real snotty, ugly cry. My mind couldn't make sense of what he'd said or what was about to go down. It had been only a week since we'd happily thrown our son's birthday party together, and a few days since he'd kissed me goodbye after a family dinner. In fact, the day before, we'd spent a beautiful afternoon at an Oktoberfest fair, and there were no signs of upset—only a close sense of family and a reminder to meet for lunch the next day.

Yet now, in the parking lot, my husband rattled off a series of reasons that he was ending our marriage. First and foremost: he didn't want to deal with any more illness and was financially drained from putting my body back together. He also insisted that I somehow caused him to develop a medical condition, which we would soon learn was a misdiagnosis, and that I was a perfectionist because I liked a clean kitchen. *Huh?* I stood there in shock, listening as the man who'd vowed to love me against all odds remorselessly stated his case for leaving our marriage. He'd given no warning that he wanted to split—not one conversation, no mention of counseling, nada. It felt as if he were stabbing me in the gut and indifferently watching me bleed; the emotional pain was so intense that it physically hurt. I couldn't reconcile the marriage that I thought I'd had for over a decade with the stranger standing before me. The whole interaction lasted about eight minutes, as if he were thoughtlessly dumping a high school fling. He then left me in the parking lot alone, sobbing so hard that a stranger pulled over to ask if I needed a ride.

Over the following weeks, I hired a lawyer and put on a good face for our son. In private, I cried like a maniac and took superlong naps. I had trouble pulling myself out of bed to shower and see friends, but I forced myself to do this (almost) daily. I ate too many Swedish fish and went for countless walks. I talked to my therapist, joined a Facebook support group with other divorced women, and picked the brains of friends whose exes had behaved similarly to mine. Yet because of my health, there was a lot that I *couldn't* do, like hitting the gym to sculpt a revenge body, smoking pot to forget my troubles, going out for drinks and getting blotto, or losing myself in hot rebound sex. I had to figure out how to work through my shit in a healthy-ish way—through no-fuss therapy that required minimal effort yet offered maximum gratification.

Then one afternoon, while waiting to meet a friend for a walk, I thought about how my therapist had urged me to write about my situation, perhaps in a memoir or essay, but a fog of sadness, fear, and anger had gotten in the way of my having much perspective on it. I also couldn't bring myself to rehash what had happened in a long and detailed account without wanting to kill my ex. I thought, *If only there were a way to vomit my feelings onto the page bluntly enough to offer relief yet briefly enough for me to escape unscathed.* I needed to vent and move on, over and over, until the agony subsided.

Suddenly, I had a flash of inspiration: haiku might just be my answer. These little poems are only three lines long, with the first and last lines having five syllables and the middle line seven. Though I'd never written any kind of poem before, I found that writing haiku landed somewhere between a thinking woman's game and a lazy woman's poetry. Processing my feelings through such short bursts of emotion also seemed like it would be more fun than the puzzles and journaling that my well-intentioned mom had suggested I do to pass the time until I miraculously healed. So, I began to write—first in the early morning before my mind reeled with relationship flashbacks, and then throughout the day whenever the mood struck. I often wrote in the middle of the night when I was too upset to sleep as well. Because so many of the early poems were fueled by unmitigated rage and a desire to shine a light on all my ex's flaws, I called them "fuck you" haiku.

In the first haiku I wrote, I mostly focused on my ex-husband, but then I started to explore how breakups make us feel in general. Friends shared their own been there/ dumped that stories that I then turned into poems, and I also scribbled about breakups from my past. I considered the various emotions and stages we go through when we end a relationship. After penning a few haiku at a time, I'd send them to friends and family for laughs and like-minded validation, deeply appreciating and reveling in the camaraderie they created between us.

For the first time since my parking-lot fiasco, I could breathe again. Haiku weren't a perfect solution to my suffering—I came to learn that only the passing of time *really* helped—but they sure were an entertaining Band-Aid. They added some levity to my painful story, and when others laughed and commiserated, it felt encouraging and supportive. Most important, I began to find my voice again, which I'd felt was taken from me when my ex unilaterally decided the fate of our family. Sure, it was only coming out three lines at a time, but at least that was something.

The end result is this ridiculous book, which I hope you'll find as amusing and therapeutic to read as it was for me to write. Though none of the poems about my ex made the final cut, the ones that did speak to the universal experiences that women go through during a breakup. Whether you enjoy a poem a day until your mood lifts, devour the book in one sitting, or feel inspired to write your own haiku is up to you. I wish you tons of love, self-assurance, and great success as you step into the next phase of your life. It might feel scary as hell, but when you take it three lines at a time, I suspect you'll at least come out on the other side with a smile.

Us

Early on in the breakup process, you can't help but reminisce about how it felt when the two of you were together. Now, the other person's absence feels palpable, like an unwanted phantom limb. When you're in bed by yourself, your foot habitually searches for theirs under the covers. You grab your phone to text them, then stop yourself mid-sentence. You consider splitting a recipe and cooking for one, but it doesn't feel worth the math. Should you even bother to finish your favorite Hulu series alone, since all you'll want to do is discuss it over leftover Chinese and a bottle of pinot?

You thought they were Your Person.

And yet . . .

A freshly cut heart can be a tricky bastard; at the start of a relationship's end, it clings to mostly sunny memories. Maybe this is how we protect ourselves from getting too upset over making an imperfect choice. Because, sure, they'd call when they said they would, but they never finished your sentences the way an other half should. And while they'd always remember your birthday, their generic gifts made you question whether they understood your desires at all.

A small voice inside likely tried to tell you that things weren't quite right, even as you told it to hush; nobody's perfect. Next time, you won't make the same mistake. Next time, you'll listen.

Our love unraveled

The universe pulled its strings

My soul knew better

You don't know a man

Until you break up with him

Ooooh, you're your father

4

It's not you, it's me

Or at least that's what I said

Of course it was you

I thought I felt seen

I gave you too much credit

You needed glasses

No pet names for me

Just pet peeves that drove me nuts

You called me "shexy"

You have a mean streak

You'd eat the last M&M

You selfish monster

You'd post pics of meals

And call yourself a foodie

I'd ring for takeout

I was full of jokes

The Sally to your Harry

It wasn't enough

You'd pee on the seat

Of our newly cleaned toilet

I never sat down

Pool, chicks, and forties

I can live without your bros

Except Tom. He's hot.

You think you're so woke

Talking politics with me

You're no Seth Meyers

We loved our tacos

You ate them in a hard shell

Pedestrian tastes

We had others fooled

I seemed the yin to your yang

We fooled ourselves, too

We were too mismatched

In retrospect, I settled

Hindsight and all that

Memories

Remember when?" stories can make you question whether the good times were ever truly valid or if the memories were just twisted, ongoing lies. Did they profess to love that trip to Anguilla as much as you did, just to be agreeable? Why would they call you "my forever" and then split a few weeks later?

What's important to know is that no matter how confusing your memories may now seem, *you have not gone mad.* No, no—you're not naïve, crazy, or foolish for trusting, believing, and investing in a person who presented themselves to you as one thing and turned out to be another. For every beautiful memory that plays in your mind, try interrupting it with a time that wasn't so hot. Hit pause on romanticizing your bond and see it for what it was. There's grace in a reality check.

Even so, keep a balanced mind. Don't doubt whether *all* the time you spent together was a mirage, because it wasn't. I believe that the memories we share with exes are real—

both the good and the bad—and that at some point our dynamic shifts, which alters the course of our relationships. This line of thinking allows you to appreciate as much as you can and let the rest go. You can then file the memories away as part of your past and be hopeful for what's coming.

All our memories

They mean nothing to you now

Tell me your secret

Under the covers

We would talk until sunrise

Now you're good as mute

You often wined me

But I can't say you dined me

Unless drunk snacks count

On Valentine's Day

I drank our Moët alone

Such a romantic

I hated driving

But road trips were your go-to

I'd eat all the snacks

You gulped fruity drinks

Bartenders thought you were lame

Pour me a double

You'd load the dishes

Like you were solving puzzles

How 'bout a hobby?

We'd host charades night

I'd point right at you: "*Clueless!*"

We won every time

I'd sleep in makeup

You'd forget to brush your teeth

How did you snag me?

You'd give lame presents

Really? A Starbucks gift card?

Thanks a latte, babe

Tried couples yoga

You'd toot in Happy Baby

That was anti-zen

I made chicken soup

When you were sick with the flu

You ate Doritos

Went to the O.C.

One of your many dull ruts

Never got to Greece

You changed overnight

Or were you always like this?

The award goes to . . .

Movie nights, sunsets

It's like they never happened

Breakup amnesia

Grief

During a breakup, we can experience deep and profound grief, just as we would with a death. It is, after all, a loss of what was. The tears come, you eat your face off, you lose yourself in friends and rebounds—lather, rinse, and repeat. Whether you stifle your sniffles behind a tissue or dramatically slide down the wall of your shower, sorrow comes in all flavors. Even months later, when you think you're improving, you'll pass your favorite brunch spot or read their first name in a book and feel like throwing up. The good news is that it does get better. It just takes a while.

Regardless of whether it was your choice to end the relationship, you will grieve. Be kind to yourself as you go through this process. You may endure months of denial, anger, depression, and bargaining before you reach acceptance. A few friends told me that once I felt disgust for my ex-husband's behavior, I'd see the light at the end of the tunnel; they were right. Cry for as long as you need to, but also fight off the rising lump in your throat. Once you know that it's possible to reduce a tidal wave of grief to a few smaller swells, you'll feel capable of doing it again. Keep yourself afloat. Anyone willing to deliberately sink your soul deserves no place in your heart.

Our tragic plot twist:

You made most things beautiful

Until you didn't

It's clear to me now

Our love never stood a chance

Under your mom's thumb

My mind won't shut off

It's impossible to sleep

You screw up my dreams

Nobody's perfect

Or that's what I tell myself

When I miss your face

I can't stop crying

I'm a salty, sloppy mess

Need beer and more beer

It's raining outside

I have no need for fresh air

Back to bed I go

A puddle of tears

And a gang of thirsty dogs

Gather at my feet

I bought dahlias

I'd hoped to cheer myself up

But we all wilted

I miss holding hands

I want to feel connected

Your skin touching mine

So much stress-eating

Cookies, popcorn, and gummies

You've ruined my thighs

You are everywhere

But the Muzak at Publix

Gets me every time

If I could reach it

I would slap my brain silly

Too much obsessing

Old habits die hard

I still sleep in your T-shirt

Consider it mine

Must get out of bed

Turn off the sappy love songs

And eat something green

Sex

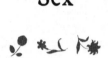

Whether sensuous or sloppy, sex memories will haunt your dreams and waking life. It's what we get for getting naked with another human being. Expect a surprising number of intimate thoughts to wash over you first thing in the morning or late at night, when your mind is quiet and still. Whether your ex explored your body with hand-here-mouth-there precision or fumbled beneath the sheets like a virgin on prom night, it doesn't much matter; your private recollections won't leave you anytime soon. Sexual experiences are like fingerprints that don't scrub off. Your body holds on to its stories, no matter how much you want a clean start.

It doesn't matter if your sex life was incredible or incredibly disappointing; you'll still feel its hollow absence. After all, you allowed another person's skin to melt into yours, and that makes you a goddess of vulnerability and desire. Embrace that unquenchable power and celebrate yourself for the temptress you are. You might feel that celebrating your sexuality makes you worthy of a deserving new person, but I think it says you deserve a goddamn crown for how you've held your own, in and out of the bedroom. But honestly, why not embrace both? You're embarking on a new life. The world is yours for the taking.

You liked what you saw

You called yourself a boob man

No more touching mine

Outside the bedroom

Our chemistry was magic

Inside, not so much

Foreplay was awkward

A tangle of arms and legs

What a sweaty mess

Your hands went to waste

Soft and smooth, with long fingers

Yet pretty clumsy

You loved to make out

Especially in public

You played to the crowd

You had weird turn-ons

Horror flicks made you randy

Call you "Freddy"? Nope.

You inhaled my mouth

Like a Hoover sucking dirt

Let's try that again

Your tongue was wiggly

Jerking like a slimy worm

That's been chopped in half

Your sex fantasies

Came from cheap porn and not love

So many hang-ups

I broke a few nails

Your back was rocky terrain

A pimply landscape

You wore ripped boxers

Yet you wanted sexy time

I had a headache

You rarely spooned me

Yet you'd poke me all night long

I'd say you forked me

You never forgot

Our dear anniversary

BJ once a year

I see you staring

Step away from my booty

It's a paws-free zone

Fights

Were all of those fights and makeups signs that your relationship was breaking down or just the ebb and flow of a partnership? You'll never know, and it doesn't matter now. Just feel grateful that you no longer have to deal with their skillfully cloaked control issues, blame games, passive-aggressiveness, gaslighting, narcissism, or [enter manipulative battle tactic here]. Focus on a brilliant future until your past spats become memories that fade away—*poof!*—one by one.

A savvy therapist once told me that "living well is the best revenge," and I think she's spot-on. Now, I know what you're thinking: the goal isn't to live your best life so that they notice, feel guilty or regretful, and come crying that they're sorry and want you back. Please don't hold your breath; if they do sniff around, it rarely lasts. This is about discovering an existence so full of happiness and free of tension that your ex no longer crosses your mind 933 times a day. Appreciating your worth, and their insignificance, becomes more satisfying than inflicting harm.

So rather than mentally replaying your relationship's Top 10 Unresolved Frustrations and Fights—always with more pointed comebacks and vengeful outcomes, I know—plot how to make life better for *you*. Go for a run so that you feel stronger and sexier in your skin. Take an epic trip and flirt with strangers in every port. Snuggle up with your best love (be it dog, child, friend . . .) and feel grateful for their affection. Being at peace trumps winning a fight any day.

All you did was blame

Because you're too weak to know

How to live your truth

Own it when you're wrong

Like they do on *Real Housewives*

You're a Ramona

You fought like a child:

"You are not the boss of me!"

Oh, go clean your room

You're angry and rude

Yet I have done nothing wrong

Other than love you

Don't call me a nag

Just because you are lazy

And your mind's a sieve

I'd wait for "sorry"

It's a futile exercise

I'd always forgive

You'd roll your brown eyes

When I'd argue a good point

You're a sore loser

You'd play the victim

But your lies were transparent

Gaslight someone else

So sneaky and snide

The villain from a cartoon

Twirling his mustache

Farewell, French mani

I bite my nails to their stubs

And spit them at you

You'd lie and then lie

You big, dumb, stupid liar

Go lie in a ditch

My name's not Oscar

You can't treat me like garbage

And think I'll take it

We'd fight in cafés

It always ended in tears

And a free dessert

You'd force the last word

To prove you were in control

Stop your mansplaining

Your stuff's in a box

On the front lawn of my house

Covered in bird shit

I swear you're broken

Couldn't piece you together

It's an inside job

Coping

There's no right or wrong way to cope, and this is not the time to judge yourself for how you're dealing with the end of your relationship. Bingeing on cheese puffs is no better or worse than bingeing on Netflix. Letting your cat gently lick your tears might be just what you need to start the day. During the thickest part of my own grief, I developed a strange affinity for old-school love songs by Neil Diamond, Air Supply, and Lionel Richie. Thankfully, nobody's going to hold you accountable for acting like the cheesiest, nerdiest, laziest, weepiest, or most maudlin version of yourself during this chaotic time.

As the kids say, you do you.

Breakups are traumatic, and trauma requires triage. If one day you need immediate care for survival, then speed-dial your closest friends until your fingers go numb. If on another day your injuries feel minor, a simple walk around the block might do. I regularly needed to bandage my wounds after my divorce, so when I took naps, I'd wrap myself in my son's bedspread as if it were an oversize dressing. The polka-dotted blanket smelled like him, which felt like love.

Just do the next sane thing until you get to the end of the day, and then do it all again. Put one furry slipper in front of the other until you're ready to face what's ahead. Let your raw and unfiltered feelings guide you all the while. They tend to take charge anyway, and that's okay.

Wine and Swedish fish

I shouldn't call that dinner

Ah, fuck it; who cares?

I hope your abs bloat

Every time I eat gluten

A pudgy one-pack

Not out for revenge

Just want you to feel like shit

There goes my karma

Redecorated

I hung a gallery wall

Completely askew

I'm a gloomy blob

Living in old, cheap leggings

Thank God for spandex

I heart dry shampoo

It's ideal during breakups

Who wants to shower?

Bingeing on Netflix

My brain is turning to goo

Can't stop watching *You*

I hang out with friends

They insist you're an asshole

Keep reminding me

Bought a voodoo doll

It's fun to stick it to you

Literally. Ouch.

I drive by your house

It doesn't count as stalking

With Mom on the phone

Built a big bonfire

Used your old clothes as kindling

Yay! More closet space.

I spin like a fiend

I'm in it for the smoothies

And hot for teacher

Facials, massages

I am all about self-care

Need to love me first

I go for long walks

The trees quietly whisper,

"You're much better off."

Building up my strength

Discovering my true north

My shrink is so proud

I need to have faith

I pray to the universe,

"Guide me to real love."

Again

It's so easy to imagine a fresh start with an old love, but I've never known good intentions and lingering attraction to carry a second act; deep love, mutual respect, dedication, and committed therapy were always required for the reunion process—and even then, the desired outcome took hard work. It's challenging to simply move on from trust that's been betrayed or questionable experiences that are *this close* to hardening into resentment. No matter how many peonies they send or cards they leave on your pillow, sometimes your future just won't include your past.

This doesn't mean that you won't try for a genuine, heartfelt do-over at least once—and that deserves credit. Many of us need to know, for sure, that we gave our relationship all we had. We need proof that it wasn't sustainable, because there's always a chance that your love *would have* prevailed. I have a lot of respect for that. It takes maturity, empathy, strength, and faith to work on a relationship and fight for love when the going gets tough. It requires character to honor a commitment and rally around a promise. Some people don't have it in them, and that's a shame.

No matter what, ending a relationship is rarely a cut-and-dried process. It's a sticky pulling apart, layered with conflicting emotions. You can want a bond to work while still questioning whether it's right for you. You can go back for a second try, wondering if their efforts are sincere. So, do and say what you need, as much as you need. Know that you've done all you can to end up where you are.

Instead of roses

You sent a dozen red flags

Cool, now my house stinks

Can we start over?

Martinis and breakup sex

Whoops, that's a mistake

One person must change

For a do-over to work

Who's it gonna be?

Put down your guitar

You're not on *The Bachelor*

Nobody's impressed

Stop calling my mom

You know she likes to meddle

Give a girl some space

I sent you a text

You said you didn't see it

Here we go again . . .

I thought we had fun

But then you—*poof!*—disappeared

Ghosts are for attics

When your mind butts in

Your intentions go to hell

Look where that leaves us

You smell like lip balm

I can taste her on your mouth

I guess that's my cue

I pluck the petals

He loves me, he loves me not

Eh, who gives a shit

You are a coward

You left without a goodbye

Good riddance to you

The mind is tricky

Could I have done something more?

No, I am enough

Reunions don't work

Not on TV, not in love

Just *The Facts of Life*

Your text makes me flinch:

"I can't do this anymore."

Yet I feel the same

Solo

You're officially single, and a novel reality is setting in. It's time to break free from any lingering funk and do what it takes to move on. Whether you called things off or were on the receiving end of your ex's baggage, there *are* bright sides to a breakup that revolve around change, creativity, and invention. Restyle your look, put together a window garden, explore your spiritual side. Crystalize what matters and reflect back to the world the person you truly are and wish to be.

Use this time between relationships to do the work and pinpoint what makes you feel valuable, genuine, and alive. Investing in yourself is always a stake that's worth the emotional and tangible effort you put into it. Clarity might come from a deep dive into that stack of self-help books hidden under your bed or snapping an elastic band that you wear on your wrist every time you linger on a harmful or discouraging thought. If you now realize that you gave too much of yourself to an ex, practice balancing what you do for others against all you should be doing for you. Everyone loves a good glow-up, but transforming yourself from the inside out creates the kind of lasting change and deep satisfaction that help inch you forward on your own best terms.

Since we ended things

The TP's always on right

Pulled from the top down

No "you" means more "me"

I'm reclaiming who I am

Happiness unfurled

I'm doing the work

Glowing from the inside out

You're watching *Borat*

The psychics all say

Your dating life is a bust

Where'd your mojo go?

I've got a new place

No Red Sox collectibles

Just my stuff, yippee!

Saw you on the street

You had toothpaste on your face

Living your best life

You hated short hair

So I chopped all of mine off

Pixie rebellion

You walked right past me

Your look was trying too hard

I tried to trip you

You seem so relieved

Bouncing around like Tigger

Take it down a notch

Goodbye, family!

I am no fan of your clan

Feeling #blessed

Now I can spread out

Sleep on the diagonal

The dogs are thrilled too

So who gets the cat?

The best consolation prize

Is a furry friend

How's this for a sign?

You left; my peace lily bloomed

Talk about bad vibes

Thought we were soul mates

That was unrealistic

Cuz you have no soul

Next

Your next chapter is about to be written, and you're poised with pen in hand. The time you spent with your ex is part of your story—a bittersweet collection of memories and moments, tidbits and tokens that you can either build on and learn from or quietly tuck away until you're ready to revisit them. How you honor or bury what remains of a past relationship is up to you.

And if your breakup continues to leave you feeling sour, please don't swear off love forever because of it. There's too much to gain from having another person tenderly crack open your heart and offer you a piece of theirs. You don't have to chase love, but do invite it in.

As thirteenth-century poet, scholar, and mystic Rumi says:

>If destiny comes to help you,
>
>Love will come to meet you.
>
>A life without love isn't a life.

Give in to the stirring and messy promise of it all. Let love come to meet you, again and again.

It's complicated

Or so you said in the end

Bullshit excuses

Sometimes love changes

But a promise should matter

Leaving is a choice

Enough is enough

I've blocked the hell out of you

Big sigh of relief

When you flew our nest

You left for a younger bird

Go barf in her mouth

You're getting married

Sorry, I lost the invite

Joke's on her this time

Can we still be friends?!

What would be the point of that?

You're deadweight to me

Click-clack go my heels

That is the sound of freedom

Me, walking away

My indifference

Is the opposite of love

A bittersweet gift

Hello, one-night stand

Shall we do your place or mine?

Right here? That works too

I've found a rebound

Got to keep my head on straight

Also, my undies

I'm in a ho phase

Is this really helping me?

Let's call it research

I'm falling again

There's a new kid on the block

Oh oh oh oh oh

If this thing is real

Gotta treat me like a queen

Or keep it movin'

Thought you'd ruined me

But you gave me a fresh start

I should say thank you

I'm in love again

Not madly, but joyfully

Here's where my heart rests

Your Turn

Inspired to claim your own poetic justice? Haiku your heart out . . .

....

....

....

....

....

....

....

....

....

Acknowledgments

I've never leaned harder on others' kindness and wisdom than I did while going through my divorce and writing these haiku as a means to cope. Breakups can be unbearably painful—and when you're drowning in heartache, it becomes obvious, really fast, who's on your side. I'm incredibly grateful for those who've made their support and love known, time and again.

Jen Bergstrom, my beloved divorce doula, I can't thank you enough for all your compassion, guidance, and friendship throughout my curious plot twist. I'm deeply grateful that you encouraged me to publish these therapeutic haiku. You are a wonderful friend and a superior doggie mom; Izzy and I are truly the luckiest gals around.

Theresa DiMasi and Lauren Hummel saw this book's potential and brought it to life. Thank you for your fabulous ideas and edits, not to mention your unwavering support. I rarely believe that relationships are meant to be, but I know the universe placed you in my path for a reason!

To my family, who've been equal parts understanding and outraged, at all the right times. Thanks for reading early drafts of these haiku and offering honest feedback, in between counseling sessions on how to get my ass out of bed and move forward with my life. Mom, thank you for always listening; Dad, your unlimited support and love have been a godsend; and Gena, you've gone above and beyond in every way. I'm lucky to have all of you in my corner.

So many friends have read and contributed to these haiku, all while holding me up emotionally. Your feedback has been funny, heartwarming, validating, and encouraging; I honestly don't know how I'd manage without you. I'd probably just snack all day and go to bed at 6:00 p.m. Nicole Bowman, Margaux Caniato, MaryAnn DiMarco, Theresa Galuszczka, Samantha Hauger, Andy Hollander, Allison Keane-Beech, Amy Lambroza, Vicky Lavergne, Emily Liebert, Pat Longo, Alia Malley, Farhad Mohammadi, Liza Neilson, Dana Parish, Alva Polinsky, and Sarah Tomalski True have been instrumental during various stages of healing and in this book's publication. I appreciate your referrals, care, and insight. You are my small army of support.

174

Vikki Stark, your life-changing therapy and mind-blowing book *Runaway Husbands: The Abandoned Wife's Guide to Recovery and Renewal* has made all the difference in my ability to understand the whys, hows, and how-could-hes and to take steps to start fresh. I'm so fortunate to have met you and your community. You are an incredibly skilled and serendipitous find.

Finally, my greatest inspiration and the motivation for all that I do is my big love, Julian. You've changed my everything and made me the happiest mama around. You're the reason I get up each day and push myself beyond measure. I love you to the asteroids and back.